Boost your business with a mark

Boost your business with a mark

Andre Marie Awoumou Manga

©**IPSA Organisation, 2013**
IPSA is an organization that promotes strategic use of Intellectual Property for personal and community development.
www.facebook.com/ipsaorg

Table of content

General introduction 7

Chapter 1 9

The notion of mark 9

    I.   Definition 9

    II.   Brief history 9

    III.   Types of marks 11

Chapter 2 15

Business idea 15

    I.   How do you find a business idea? 15

    II.   How do you identify a great business idea? ...19

    III.   By which means do you get your product? .20

Chapter 3 25

The function of the mark for an entrepreneur 25

    I.   The mark produces money 25

    II.   The mark preserves the money of the trader from diversion and loss 27

Chapter 4 35

How do you collect money from your mark? 35

I.	Exploitation of a mark	35
II.	Protection of the mark	40

Chapter 5 47

Acquisition of a mark 47

I.	Criteria of registration	47
II.	Criteria of efficiency	50
III.	Copyright issues	53

Annex I – Useful websites 55

Annexe II : Internet adresses of National and Regional Intellectual Property offices.................57

Annex III – Nice Classification: International Classification of Goods and Services for the Purposes of the Registration of Marks under the Nice Agreement 67

Bibliography...77

General introduction

Nowadays, a mark is vital for an entrepreneur; it is almost an indispensable asset to survive and grow in the market place. In fact the mark is at the heart of brand which importance in an economic context of world economy and free market is highlighted by Veernan Nidlanavong, deputy Director of Thailand's Department of Industrial Promotion, when he says: *"We operate in a highly competitive global market flooded with many similar products. Developing a brand that effectively communicates the origin of a product, its quality and the local materials and know-how used to produce it, as well as the identity of the producer, is a key element in making products more competitive and marketable."* In the same line of thought Disney CEO Michael Eisner argues: *"When the choices have become vast, the only things that will matter are brand names".*

Being an entrepreneur is all about bringing a solution to a certain public's need in the market place in the form of a product, making sure those who may be interested in your product know about it, and making sure the product is always sufficiently available in the market place. The key of the success in such an undertaking is branding i.e. the process of communication that generates a certain image for a product in the consumers' mind and that aims to persuade them to pay for the product. It has been said that "branding is one of the most powerful tools to strengthen the marketing power of products"[1].

So the best attitude to succeed in "consumer focused" business is to be "brand focused" from the conception of the business idea to production and commercialization of products. At the same time, communication you address to the public to generate a certain image for your product and to convince them to pay for your product is mainly supported or made possible by your trademark or service mark. So, the mark is the bedrock of brand to the point that sometimes the two concepts mean the same thing. In other words, branding is coming up with a convincing and persuasive trademark or service mark.

---

[1] Project on Intellectual Property and Product Branding for Business development in developing countries and Least-developed Countries (LDCS)

Chapter 1

The notion of mark

I. Definition

The mark is an intellectual property asset defined by the World intellectual Property Organization (WIPO) as « a distinctive sign, which identifies certain goods or services as those produced or provided by a specific person or enterprise. »[2] It has also been defined as "any sign, or any combination of signs, capable of distinguishing the goods or services of one undertaking from those of other undertakings"[3]

II. Brief history

In those days when production was essentially local and the notion of competition was not developed, the mark was simply a "signal". As such, they were used to provide an automatic response that could help to identify the marker of the product. Precisely, they were applied for further claim of ownership[4]. So, farmers could recognize their animals in case of mixture of livestock.

---

[2] WIPO publication N'450(E)
[3] Article 15 (1) of the TRIPS Agreement
[4] Lionel Bently and Brad Sherman, *Intellectual Property Law* (2009), 712

Merchants also could retrieve their goods in case of confusing situation (shipwreck for example). In the medieval times, the Guilds changed slightly the use of the mark[5]. They were a trade organization that controlled the quality of products. They required their members to apply identifying marks or signs to the goods, so they could easily identify the source of unsatisfactory goods.

With the industrial revolution, the need to conquer market share was more pressing, sometimes far from the headquarters of the traders. The transnational trading grew and competition started to dictate its law[6]. There was a need to orientate or convince the public; it became the new role of trademark that was accentuated by the growth of mass media and the reading public. Trademark was henceforth a witness of quality and a tool of advertising[7]; a tool of communication between the trader and the public. That's how we moved from trademark as 'signal" to trademark as "symbol"[8]. Trademark became "a poetic device, a

---

[5] P.Mollerup, *Marks of excellence: The history and taxonomy of Trademarks* (1997) 15-42; S.Diamond, "The historical Development of trademarks" (1975) 65 TM Rep 265, 272

[6] B.Pattishal, "Trade marks and the Monopoly Phobia" (1952) 42 *TM Rep* 588, 590-1.

[7] Development of advertising has reinforced the role of mark as an instrument used to identify the commercial origin of a product. Diamond, "Historical Development of trademarks", 281.

[8] Dresche, « transformation and evolution of trademarks ».

name designed to conjure up product attributes whether real or imagined"[9].

Recently, a new function of trademark has been identified. They provide customers with an identity. In fact, some trademarks have generated such an aura that they have reached the mythical dimension[10] where they are considered by consumers as a way of live. In France, there are for example some people who define themselves as Citroen driver resulting to the creation of associations of Citroen drivers. But, more than a function, this seems to be the new result of the use of trademarks as both a tool of communication and marketing.

III. Types of marks

Nowadays, we find several types of marks in the marketplace:

Trade marks are used to distinguish certain goods as those produced by a specific enterprise.

Service marks are used to distinguish certain services as those provided by a specific enterprise. Services may be of any kind, such as financial, banking, travel, advertising or catering, to name a few. Service marks can be registered,

---

[9] Ibid, 338
[10] Dresher, "transformation and evolution of trademarks". The expression "mythical status" is rather used

renewed, cancelled, assigned and licensed under the same conditions as trademarks.

A **collective mark** is generally owned by an association or cooperative whose members may use the collective mark to market their products. The association generally establishes a set of criteria for using the collective mark (e.g., quality standards) and permits individual companies to use the mark if they comply with such standards. Collective marks may be an effective way of jointly marketing the products of a group of enterprises which may find it more difficult for their individual marks to be recognized by consumers and/or handled by the main distributors.

Certification marks are given for compliance with defined standards, but are not confined to any membership. They may be used by anyone whose products meet certain established standards. In many countries, the main difference between collective marks and certification marks is that the former may only be used by a specific group of enterprises, e.g., members of an association, while certification marks may be used by anybody who complies with the standards defined by the owner of the certification mark.

Well-known marks are marks that are considered to be well-known by the competent authority of the country where protection for the mark is sought. Well-known marks generally benefit from stronger protection. For example, well-known marks may be protected even if they are not registered (or have not even been used) in a given territory

Chapter 2

Business idea

I. How do you find a business idea?

A. *The initial task of an entrepreneur*

Some people think they cannot succeed in business. But whoever you are, if you have ever solved somebody's problem, or you know how to solve somebody's problem, you may find your way in the market place; it is just a matter of investment and strategy. The solution you provide for a specific problem is your product; it may be a good or a service. You just need to identify other people who face the same problem, make sure that they know about your product and that they can access it. The more they are, the more you succeed.

We can agree with Boynton that "At any given time, there's a job that has to get done". In daily life, they are jobs that others have abandoned, ignored, or failed to address effectively…the world is full of problems that need to be solved. Those problems can be solved by a given good or service, a specific technique or process to manufacture a given product, a specific way to promote or distribute a given product, a way to offer a service…

So, the initial task of an entrepreneur is to find a solution to a need for a given public, and this is not a magical issue!

B. Approaches to come up with business idea

To find a solution to people need, and so come up with a business idea, you may invent a product, acquire the authorization to exploit a patented product owned by somebody else, purchase a product owned by somebody else, or simply exploit an existing non protected product…

There are two mains approaches to come up with business idea:

- *You first find a product*

You may discover a product in a dedicated website or magazine for business ideas, in the market place, in a patent document…A potential partner or seller may come to you with a product (it may be an inventor, an owner of patented invention, promoter of a product, an entrepreneur...); you may have a certain know-how or skill…

In those cases you have to ask yourself: "can this know-how or product solve a given problem in the society? If yes who may need it?"

- ***You first identify a problem or a need in the society***

The second approach to come up with business idea is to first Identify a need in the society and then to find a solution to it. You may invent a product, search how the same problem is solved elsewhere, contact R&D institutions, design a service…

An interesting source of inspiration for a business idea is then people you encounter. Observe them and ask yourself: what bug them? What are their frustrations? What can be easier for them? What can be more convenient for them? Observe what they consume or use, is there any possibility to improve it? It has been said that "you are surrounded by problems that someone has tried to solve. Each is an opportunity to learn. Start noticing how convenience stores organize inventory, how packaging catches your eye, or how Amazon encourages impulse buys. You might find a better way to solve the same problem or inspiration for solving a different problem". The questions above may also efficiently apply to yourself; that's why Boynton says: "Start with your own experience". There are certainly other people who have the same needs as you.

Let's consider the imagined case of John. After moving into his new neighborhood, he went to an internet cafe. Unfortunately, he spent three quarters of his time waiting for pages he was trying to visit to display. He noted that other clients were complaining of the same problem of slow connection. The next day, he returned in the same internet cafe and suffers the same inconvenience. He then went to another internet cafe in the same neighborhood, it was not better at all! He realized that in this area there was a pressing need of "a fast connection that would actually allow customers to effectively work for the time they buy." The business idea was born. This connection that was intended to improve the lives of users was the product that john has the challenge to bring to the market place to effectively establish his business.

    Now, let's examine how the myth Coca-Cola started. Colonel John Pemberton was wounded in the civil war. He became addicted to morphine which he was using to relieve his pain. But as he dreaded the effect of that drug, he began a quest to find a substitute. Meanwhile, he became a pharmacist. He started making researches, that's how he invented the formula of "a drink with therapeutic virtues"; this was the "first live of Coca-cola" which has not been that successful. Asa Candler, believed in that project, not as a drug, but simply as a "Carbonated soft drink with special taste". He managed to acquire the exclusive rights on it and started an aggressive marketing.

II. How do you identify a great business idea?

We have already said that if your business is consumer focused your better chance to survive in the marketplace is branding. So you should arrange for branding from your business idea, it should then be a branding-receptive business idea.

An entrepreneur fundamentally has to bear in mind that other are trying or will try to make money in the same field as him. In such an environment of competition, the success of a business depends on its capacity to be supported by a mark which will allow efficient branding. In fact, the mark is a mean to select and bring a solution to people needs in the market place in the form of products. The public in turn appreciate the capacity of a product to satisfy his need, and associate that capacity to the mark, that is how the mark acquires reputation and becomes a cash dispenser. The bedrock of a successful mark is then a convincing specific solution to people need in the society; it may be a particular product, a particular technique to produce, to distribute, and to market a given product, a way to offer a service…

At the very beginning of his project, considering his targeted public, an entrepreneur has to ask himself: «what is proposed to the public in this particular field? », « how will I distinguish from my competitors? », « how do I want the public to talk about my mark? ». The objective of those questions is to master on what his reputation will be built and advertising based; the intended particularity of his mark in the market place, the base of branding.

III. By which means do you get your product?

A. Invention

In Intellectual Property Jargon, "an invention is generally defined as a new and inventive solution to a technical problem."[11] An invention may relate to the creation of an entirely new device, product, method or process.

They say you have invented a product or process when you come up with a product or a process that is not already known as part of the prior art (Novelty requirement for patentability) and that is not obvious to a person with ordinary skill in the field considered (Non-obviousness requirement for patentability). This obviously requires a certain capacity that is enhanced by knowledge in a given scientific or technology area. The said knowledge can be acquired through education or training at

---

[11] *Inventing the Future; An introduction to patents for Small and Medium-Sized Enterprises*, World Intellectual Property Organization, Publication No 917 (E), 2006

research and development institutions, technical institutes or centers of higher learning. This Knowledge can also be acquired through study of books, periodicals or other publications on special scientific and technical subjects, or read patent documents.

To be patentable, apart from novelty and non-obviousness requirement, an invention must consist of patentable subject matter and be industrially applicable or simply useful.

An invention doesn't consist of patentable subject matter when it is expressly excluded for patentability by the national law. The following are generally excluded from patentability: discoveries and scientific theories; aesthetic creations; schemes, rules and methods for performing mental acts; mere discoveries as they naturally occur in the world; inventions that may affect public order, good morals or public health; diagnostic, therapeutic and surgical methods of treatment for humans or animals; plants and animals other than microorganisms, and essentially biological processes for the production of plants or animals other than non-biological and microbiological processes; computer programs.

The industrially applicable requirement means that the invention can be applied for practical purposes, not be purely theoretical. If the invention is intended to be a product, it should be possible to make that product. And if the invention is intended to be a process or part of a process, it should be possible to carry that process out or "use" it practice.

B. License of patent

License is a contractual agreement through which a legal entity or a person is granted the permission by the owner of a patented invention to perform, in a given country for a certain period of time, one or more of the acts which are covered by the exclusive rights to the patented invention, in exchange of negotiated compensation (royalties, advantages…)

In other words, a license is a legal mean for an entrepreneur to acquire rights from the owner of a patent to manufacture his invention, to manufacture a product that embodies the invention, to make products by a process that includes the invention…

"Licensing is particularly useful if the company that owns the invention is not in a position to make the product at all or in sufficient quantity to meet a given market need, or to cover a given geographical area."[12]

"As a license agreement requires skillful negotiations and drafting, it is advisable to seek the

---

[12] *Inventing the Future; An introduction to patents for Small and Medium-Sized Enterprises*, World Intellectual Property Organization, Publication No 917 (E), 2006

assistance of a licensing practitioner for negotiating the terms and conditions and for drafting the licensing agreement."

C. Assignment of patent

Assignment is a contractual agreement through which the owner of a patented invention, the assignor, sales his exclusive rights on that invention to another party, the assignee.

So, with an assignment, the owner of the patented invention transfer to you all his exclusive rights without any restriction in time or other condition.

Assignment is a solution for an entrepreneur who finds a business idea which is not yet exploited by the owner or in the case where the owner seems unable to exploit it normally.

D. Franchising

A franchise or distributorship is a business arrangement whereby a license of a mark or a name of one enterprise called franchisor to another called franchisee is combined with the supply of know-how in some form, either technical information, technical services, technical assistance or management services concerning production, marketing, maintenance and administration.

The particularity of a franchising arrangement is that the franchisor keeps control of his brand. He allows the franchisee to represent his brand and sell his product or render his services in a given geographic area.

Franchising is designed for an entrepreneur who wants to exploit the reputation and the marketing know-how of a well-known mark in a geographical area where it is not yet available.

Chapter 3

The function of the mark for an entrepreneur

Nowadays, the mark is essentially a tool that targets the consumer in order to transmit a message or to offer an identity. The ultimate goal of this is simply to extract money from his wallet. Such a tool is critical for the trader in the world context of market economy dominated by rude competition because it determines the amount of money he collects in the market place. We can then say that the ultimate function of the mark for an entrepreneur is to provide him with money.

The mark is simply the Cash dispenser of the trader to the extent that it produces money for him through its use and at the same time protects that money from diversion by any third party and from loss thanks to its system of protection.

I. The mark produces money

In the market place nowadays, the consumer is faced with several choices. Most of the time, he does not have neither time nor means to test the products or to get appropriate information about their qualities before purchasing. He then has to take risks and trust a particular product. To decide, he necessarily needs to rely on an element which allows him to quickly apply his rational judgment or emotional preference. This element is often offered by the trader and it is the trademark.

The mark is first of all a tool of communication directed to the consumer. It has been said that "where the quality and/or variety of goods is not readily apparent, trademarks enable consumers to choose the product with the desired features" and that the trademark "facilitate and enhance consumer decisions". The trademark user says to the public:" I have created, invented, produced, or selected this specific product for you…this product has the same quality or know how that the other one you liked in the past or the one you heard about". The trader uses his mark to build his reputation and goodwill, based on its ability to forward a message of quality.

The mark can also convey an emotion to the potential consumer. So, by the virtue of it distinctiveness or appeal, it attracts customers. This is known as "advertising" quality of the mark. The trader can however collect more customers by increasing advertising through the manipulation of his sign. American academic Ralph Brown said rightly: "advertising depends on remote manipulation of symbols, most importantly of symbols directed at a mass audience through mass media or imprinted on mass-produced goods. The essence of these symbols is distilled in the devices variously called trademarks, trade names, brand names or brand symbols". So the mark helps the user through advertising to gather more quickly and massively customers. Sometimes, the promotion done through the mark generates a very powerful aura that is persuasive in itself. The choice is then no longer rational[13], but based on the "psychological hold"[14] exerted by the mark on the consumer.

II. The mark preserves the money of the trader from diversion and loss

As we said earlier, if the use of the mark provides the user with money, its protection preserves diversion and loss of that money. Actually, the system of protection of marks aims to avoid revenue shortfalls and to secure further possible income. In fact the Intellectual property rights are often referred to as negative rights in a sense that they grant the owner of intellectual property asset the right to exclude any third party from the exploitation of their asset[15]. However, the

---

[13] E.g. Kur (1992) 23 I.I.C. 218; Martino, *Trade Mark Dilution* (1996); Mostert, *Famous and well-known* Marks (1997); McCarthy in Vaver and Bently Ch.11.

[14] Griffiths (2011) I.P.Q. 326 at 329. Griffiths claims that trademarks "can gain a "psychological hold" on the minds of consumers, which gives them a selling power above that of the underlying goodwill".

[15] See article 16 of the TRIPS Agreement (1994)

actual goal of this right is not to prevent the use of the asset as such; but to make sure that all its uses benefit the owner and are made in accordance with him. The trademark protection system protects the owner's incomes, real and potential. To this end, relying on trademark infringement and in some cases passing off action or unfair competition law, it usually combats some harmful situations to the portfolio of the trader caused by the action of non unauthorized users of the sign, namely, diversion of trade, harm to reputation, dilution, loss of possibility for the trader to extend his activities in new fields or geographical areas, loss of sources of income inherent to the trademark. More precisely:

- **The mark protection system aims to combat misrepresentation generating confusion about source or origin of goods or services and diverting trade**

The Union for the protection of industrial property[16] decided "to refuse or to cancel the registration, and to prohibit the use," of trademarks liable to create confusion[17]. According to the same Union, this may occur in case of reproduction, imitation, and translation of existing trademark. A concrete example of such a confusing situation

---

[16] The Union for the protection of industrial property is constituted by the countries to which the Paris Convention applies.
[17] See article 6bis Paris Convention

constituting trademark infringement is counterfeiting[18] I.e. imitation of a product giving the impression of being a genuine one originating from the genuine manufacturer or trader[19]. Another example is imitation of labels and packaging[20], where unlike counterfeiting, the imitation does not give the impression of being the genuine product. Generally trading under his own name, the liable competitor simply tries to take advantage of existing trademark by using a trademark that is confusingly similar or that is likely to suggest a link with the later. This is of course also a case of unfair competition.

- **The mark protection system aims to avoid loss of possibility to extend business in new fields or geographical areas**

Trademark is money. But collection of that money relies on the capacity of the owner which in turn depends on factors such as management, investment, efficiency in distribution… So this capacity is increased as the user explores new markets. In the logic of trademark protection system, the owner should not lose the possibility to expand into a new field or a new geographic area

---

[18] See article 6bis Paris Convention
[19] See WIPO Intellectual Property Handbook, Second edition, P 90.
[20] See WIPO Intellectual Property Handbook, Second edition, P 91.

because a non authorized third party already uses his mark. This furthermore would be a loss of potential income. Piracy thus constitutes an infringement to trademark[21]. There is trademark piracy where a person registers or uses a generally well-known trademark in a country where the said mark is not registered or is invalid as result of non-use without the authorization of the owner[22].

- **The mark protection system aims to avoid loss of possibility of licensing or assignment**

The fact that unauthorized use of the trademark by third party, particularly piracy, is an infringement is important for the trademark owner at more than one level. It helps amongst others to protect two very important potential sources of income, namely, licensing and assignment. In fact, the trademark law grants the trademark owner the possibility to monetize the use of his mark where he does not have the ability to exploit it himself or where he considers someone else better equipped. This is achievable through licensing and assignment that are mechanisms through which the trademark owner entrust its exploitation to a third party.

---

[21] See article 6bis Paris Convention
[22] See WIPO Intellectual Property Handbook, Second edition, P 90 for the definition of piracy.

- **The mark protection system aims to prevent third party to harm the reputation of the mark**

Proposing lower quality goods or services under the umbrella of a mark is definitely very harmful for the reputation. The fact that the trademark owner is basically the only person who can authorize the use of his mark precisely allow him to control what is offered under it. Let us note that "in contrast with other areas of intellectual property law such as designs, copyright, and patents, there are no compulsory licenses in relation to trademarks"[23]. Third party can lawfully authorize another third party to use the mark if and only if they have acquired this power from the owner, inter alia, through assignment or exclusive license. So the trademark owner can at the outset exclude those who do not satisfy his interests from the use of his sign, foremost among them those who cannot offer products with a level of quality required. Moreover, in case of license, a certain quality standard may be imposed to the licensee. If this may be done by virtue of the law in some countries like the USA and Sri Lanka, it may also be done by control provisions in a recorded agreement.

The unfair competition law also helps to protect the reputation of a trader. So under it, article

---

[23] Lionel Bently and Brad Sherman, *Intellectual Property Law* (2009), 967

10bis (3) of the Paris convention prohibits "false allegations in the course of trade of such a nature as to discredit the establishment, the goods, or the industrial or commercial activities, of a competitor".

- **The mark protection system aims to prevent loss of possibility to increase the reputation because of dilution**

The law has also identified dilution as a situation that affects the profitability of a mark. It is characterized by the fact that the mark can no longer sustain the reputation of the trader. This occurs where improper use causes the mark to become familiar or commonplace and, as a result, undetermined the ability of the sign to summon up particular goods or values; it can then be said that the sign has become generic. Dilution due to misrepresentation by third party is recognized by the courts as form of damage.

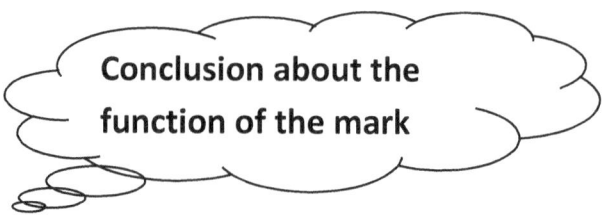

Conclusion about the function of the mark

From the use of the mark nowadays emerges a major observation: it is essentially a tool that targets the consumer in order to transmit a message or to offer an identity. The ultimate goal of this is simply to extract money from his wallet through exploitation of the reputation and the aura acquired by the mark in the market place. The quality of the offer and advertising are then key factors for a mark to provide money to its user. To maximize his profit, a system of protection is built to protect that money, real or potential, from diversion by third party. In the world context of market economy where the choices are so vast, the mark is vital for a trader as it determines the amount of money he collects in the market place; it is simply his cash dispenser.

Chapter 4

How do you collect money from your mark?

You collect money from you mark through its exploitation and its protection.

I. Exploitation of a mark

Self exploitation

The owner of a mark can exploit his mark himself. This means that he uses the mark to offer to the public the products he selects. Those products may be produced or created by him or by his business partner.

The mark helps him to distinguish his offer in the market place, to benefit from the reputation acquired thanks to his skill and the image generated through advertising. So, in the course of trade, he affixes the sign to his goods or to packaging thereof; offers or exposes goods for sale, puts them on the market or stocks them for these purposes under the sign, or offers or supplies services under the sign; imports or exports goods under the sign; uses the sign on business papers or in advertising.

A company may have various trademarks. For instance, Nestlé S.A. has Nestlé, Nido, Milo,

Nescafé... Companies may use a specific trademark to identify all their products. This generally aims to indicate the link with that mark, so that all the products, specifically new ones, can benefit from its reputation. For instance you find the mark Nestlé on almost all the products manufactured by Nestlé S.A. Companies may also use a specific trademark to identify a particular range of products or one specific type of product (Nestlé S.A. use Nescafé for coffee, Nido for milk...)

Some companies may also use their trade name, or a part of it, as a trademark (Nestlé S.A. uses Nestlé as trademark). They should, in that case, register it as a trademark.

Figure 1: Nido, a trademark used by Nestlé S.A. for milk. The trade mark Nestlé is also applied on the product to show the link with Nestlé S.A

Figure 2: Ricoré, a trademark used by Nestlé S.A for coffee. The mark Nestlé is also applied to show the link with Nestlé S.A

B. Exploitation by a third party

The owner of the mark can also entrust its exploitation to a third party through assignment, licensing, or franchising. In this case, he benefits from royalties or lump sum primarily negotiated. This offers him the possibility to make profits from his mark even in an area or field where he does not have the ability to exploit it himself or where he considers someone else better equipped for this exploitation. Rightly, assignment, licensing and franchising may be limited geographically, in relation to particular goods or services, or as to manner of use. In addition, the licensing and franchising may be limited temporarily.

Let's just point out by the way that basically, while an assignment is a transfer of ownership of the trade mark, license is merely the permission to use it. This normally implies some differences as to the rights and responsibilities of each party involved in the operation, depending on the case (assignor/assignee; licensor/licensee). But the laws and usages have evolved so that sometimes, licensing is a quasi transfer of ownership.

"The licensing of a trademark is central to a franchising agreement. In franchising agreements the degree of control of the trademark owner over the franchisee is generally greater than is the case for standard trademark licensing agreements. In the case of franchising, the franchiser allows another person (the franchisee) to use his way of doing business (including trademarks, know-how, customer service, software, shop decoration, etc.) in accordance with a set of prescriptions and in exchange for compensation or royalty."

C. Use of the mark as mortgage

"A carefully selected and nurtured trademark is a valuable business asset for most companies. For some, it may be the most valuable asset they own. Estimates of the value of some of the world's most famous trademarks such as Coca-Cola or IBM exceed 50 billion dollars each. This is because consumers value trademarks, their reputation, their image and a set of desired qualities they associate with the mark, and are willing to pay more for a product bearing a trademark that they recognize and which meets their expectations. Therefore, the very ownership of a trademark with a good image and reputation provides a company with a competitive edge."

Trademark may then be used as security for a debt. "This can be a useful technique to enable the proprietors of trade marks to raise funds". Practically, the mortgagor-borrower assigns (transfer the ownership of) his mark to the mortgagee-lender in exchange for money, while providing in the transaction a mechanism allowing him to retrieve his property once the debt is paid.

This mechanism may be reassignment, redemption, exclusive license... "Another alternative is to subject the trademark to 'a charge", in which case there is no assignment. Instead, the chargee gains certain rights over the trademark".

II. Protection of the mark

The owner of a mark should understand its Protection as any action that prevents him from loosing the money provided by his mark, real or potential. Thus, the protection of a mark is a wide concept that encompasses protection of ownership, protection of distinctiveness, protection of reputation.

Protection of ownership and rights

The owner of a mark is granted exclusive rights on it, in other word the right to exclude third party from the use of his mark without his authorization[24]. Secure such a prerogative is fundamental if the trader want to build his reputation, collect money from his mark and prevent the diversion of money by third party.

Historically, two systems have developed: one granted the ownership and thus the protection to the first trader to use the mark and the other granted it to the first to register the mark. But nowadays, as the Paris Convention places contracting countries

---

[24] See article 16 (1) TRIPS Agreement (1994)

under the obligation to provide for a trademark register, "full trademark protection is properly secured only by registration"[25].

But despite the generalization of the registration, the use of the sign remains a determining factor for protection. Indeed, the non use of the mark after a grace period[26] following the registration may lead to cancellation at the request of a person with a legitimate interest. In addition, if the registration grants the right to exclude other from the use of the mark, its non use gives the right to other to exclude the registrant from the use of his mark. The importance given to the use in the process of protecting the mark is inherent to the function of this later. Basically, the function of the mark is to distinguish the goods on which the trademark is registered from others. What would be the purpose of protection if there is no product to distinguish! "It makes no economic sense, therefore, to protect trademarks by registration without imposing the obligation to use them.

Ultimately, it is not enough to register a mark, it is fundamental to be ready to use it.

---

[25] WIPO (World Intellectual Property Organisation), WIPO Intellectual Property Hand Book (WIPO Publication No 489(E), 2008

[26] A grace period is generally granted in trademark laws, providing for a use obligation tree or five years after filing application.

Registration of trade name

Registration of a trade name at the business registry does not imply its registration as a trademark. The aim of the registration of a trade name is to legalize a business. A trade name is the full name of your business, such as: "Blackmark International Ltd" and it identifies your company. It often ends with Ltd, Inc, S.A, SARL or other similar abbreviations that denote the legal character of the company. But a trade name may also be registered as a trademark, and this implies a different procedure in front of

The loss of ownership of a mark may also occur if the owner doesn't renew the mark or if he doesn't use it for a certain period of time specified in the relevant trademark law.

B. Protection of distinctiveness

The user of a mark has to bear in mind that the mark is a tool that helps him to distinguish his products or services from others in the market place. Without that function, he cannot benefit from any reputation in the market place, he cannot benefit from advertising, and his efforts to maintain certain quality standard for his offer will be useless.

To maintain distinctiveness, transformation of the mark into a generic term should be avoided. Therefore the use of the mark must never allow ambiguity to the public on the fact that the mark identifies a specific product as one in a certain category. To this end, some rules should be observed:

- It is first of all important to ensure "there is already a generic name for the branded good or service in question, even if the name has to be invented by the trademark owner – which could well be the case with a unique new product. Examples include "correction fluid" for liquid WITE-OUT products." This generic name should always accompany the mark.

- The mark should not be used as, or instead of, the product designation.

- The mark should never be used with an article, and the possessive "s" and the plural form should be avoided

- The mark should always be highlighted

- The mark should be identified as such by a trademark notice

- The so-called "Health maintenance program" may sometimes be useful. It is all about running advertisements to remind the public the marks are not generic names and should not be used as such. Generally, such advertisements target writers and editors.

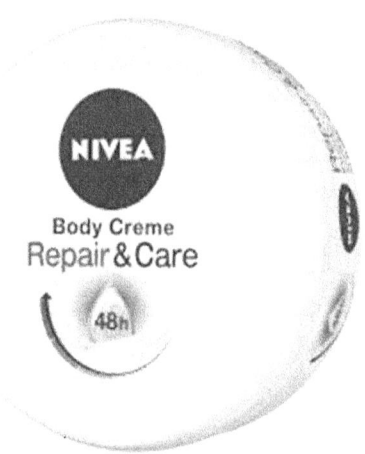

Figure 3: Nivea, a well-known trademark. We can see how they apply their trademark on their product

C. *Protection of reputation*

It has been said that the marks « create incentives for firms to produce products of desirable qualities… »[27]. Indeed, the success of a mark

---

[27] Economides, « Economics of Trademarks », 526-6. Landes and Posner, « Economics of Trademark Law », 270. See also A. Griffiths, « The law and Economics of Trade Marks » in Bently, Davis & Ginsburg Ch 11; J.Aldred, « The Economic Rationale for Trade Marks: An Economist's Critique », ibid, ch 12.

fundamentally depends on the quality of the products offered under it. It has also been said that "What consumers understand by the mark will depend on their previous knowledge and experience"[28]. In fact, if the quality of a product is not satisfactory, the purchasers will be disappointed and this is very harmful for reputation. If on the contrary a consumer is satisfied by a product he purchases, he will have a tendency in his next purchases to seek the products offered by the same trader or to advise them to others referring to its mark, so he associates somehow that mark to quality or satisfaction.

The quality of the offer is the bedrock of the reputation because it determines the client's decision to return buy the products of the same brand or to advise them to another person. This obliges the user of a mark to maintain a certain standard for his offer.

---

[28] Cornish, Llewelyn and Aplin, Intellectual Property: Patents, Copyright, Trade Marks and Allied Rights seventh edn (2010), p 637

Chapter 5

Acquisition of a mark

Criteria of registration

Generally speaking, any sign capable of distinguishing the goods or services of one undertaking from those of other undertaking may be a mark. However, the registration of a mark is subject to some requirements:

- Nature of the sign

Most often, only signs that can be represented graphically are registrable as trademarks; this is the rule in most countries. It may be: Words or sets of words (whether invented or not: names, surnames, forenames, geographical names, fanciful words, slogans…), Letters And Numerals (one or more letters, one or more numerals or any combination thereof), Combinations of any of those listed above; Logotypes and labels, Colors or combinations of colors (applied on devices, packaging, words…), Three-Dimensional Signs (shape of the goods or their packaging, any tree dimensional representation…)

Some legislation may admit Audible Signs (Sound Marks: musical notes, cry of an animal…),

Olfactory Marks (Smell Marks), Other (invisible) Signs…

- The sign should be distinctive

Generally, there is lack of distinctiveness where the sign have a generalist nature leading to the fact that other traders have the legitimate interest in its fair use. A trader has no interest to use such a sign as trademark if he wants to acquire market share. Even if it has been demonstrated that with intensive use they may acquire a secondary meaning finally making them distinctive, it is risky to bet on such signs because reaching there is costly in terms of money and time, and because for the interest of both trade and consumers many countries don't allow any particular trader to monopolize them through registration. This is especially the case where the sign is generic or descriptive. A generic sign defines a category or type of product. As an example, the term "handicraft" cannot be used as a trademark by an artisan who produces handicrafts. Descriptive signs on the other hand "designate the kind, quality, intended purpose, value, and place of origin, time of production or any other characteristic of the goods for which the sign is intended to be used or is being used".

There is also lack of distinctiveness where the sign is not able to capture the consumer's attention as a sign referring to the origin of the product because it melts on the packaging or is not detectable as a distinctive sign. This can happen if the sign is too simple or appears as a pure illustration or ornament or is in the form of a too long advertising slogan that finally becomes too much complex to be understood by consumers as reference to the origin of the product.

- The sign should not be deceptive

Let us specify that the deception referred to here is the intrinsic deception, inherent in the trademark itself when associated with the goods for which it is proposed. It is established where it is proved that the mark misleads the consumer as to the nature, quality or any other characteristics of the goods or their geographical origin.

- The sign should not be contrary to morality or public interest.

- The sign should not be an imitation of existing mark

Irrespective of the type of mark you choose, it is important to avoid imitating existing trademarks. A slightly altered competitor's trademark or a misspelt well-known or famous mark is unlikely to be registered. Example: EASY WEAR is a registered trademark for teenage clothing. It would be unwise to try to sell the same or similar products using the trademark EEZYWARE as it would probably be considered confusingly similar to the existing mark and is unlikely to be registered.

- Signs excluded from registration

Flags, armorial bearings, official hallmarks and emblems of states and international organizations which have been communicated to the International Bureau of WIPO are usually excluded from registration

II. Criteria of efficiency

An efficient mark produces money. It should then allow the public to find the products of the trader; it should also convey reputation and support advertising. More precisely:

- The sign should be distinctive

Distinctiveness is not simply a legal criteria for registration; it is a necessity for the success of a mark. In fact, it is fundamentally important that the sign used as mark enables the consumer to identify the trader's products or services amongst different offers. Without distinctiveness, the mark can neither convey the reputation due to the quality of the offer, nor be efficient tool of advertising.

- Suggestiveness may be an advantage

A suggestive sign generates a positive association with the product in the mind of the consumer. Such sign is neither totally arbitrary nor clearly descriptive. It subtly refers to nature, quality, origin or any other characteristic of the goods they are applied for. The appeal of suggestive marks is that they act as a form of advertising. A slight risk, however, is that some countries may consider a suggestive mark to be too descriptive of the product and thus may not register it Example: The trademark SUNNY for marketing electric heaters would hint at the fact that the product is meant to radiate heat and keep your house warm.

- Appeal

The artistic qualities of a mark and it suggestiveness play an important role for its appeal. It is said that some marks, by virtue of their appeal, are able to convey some sort of emotional allure to potential consumers. This is known as "advertising quality" of the mark. So by itself, the mark attracts consumers.

- The sign should not be repellent

It should be easy to read, write, spell and remember. It should not have any undesired connotations in your own language or in any of the languages of potential export markets.

- A suitable sign is suitable to all types of advertising media.
- The corresponding domain name (i.e. Internet address) should be available for registration

Discussion: Implication of certain types of words

Coined or "fanciful" words: these are invented words without any intrinsic or real meaning. Coined words have the advantage of being easy to protect, as they are more likely to be considered inherently distinctive. On the negative side, however, they may be more difficult to remember for consumers, requiring greater effort to advertise the products.

Arbitrary marks: these are words that have a meaning that has no relation to the product they advertise. While these types of marks will also be easy to protect, they may also require heavy advertising to create the association between the mark and the product in the minds of consumers.

Suggestive marks: these are marks that hint at one or some of the attributes of the product. The appeal of suggestive marks is that they act as a form of advertising. A slight risk, however, is that some countries may consider a suggestive mark to be too descriptive of the product.

III. Copyright issues

Selecting or creating an appropriate mark is a critical step, as it is an important element of the marketing strategy of your business. The mark generally consists on an artistic or literary work. You may not have the creative skill to design the appropriate mark. There are, in fact, specialized companies whose main service is to find or develop an appropriate trademark for your needs. You may also entrust the task to your employee.

A. Commissioned mark

A commissioned work is a work created by one person for another person. Specifically, a person contacts an author or a specialized company and asks him to create a work on his behalf. Both parties are bound by an express or implied contract to create a work.

In some countries (civil law countries most of the time), a commissioned work belongs to the author or co-authors, but property rights are often automatically transferred to the commissioner. This means that once the work delivered, it is the commissioner who now has the exclusive right to reproduce, adapt, translate, to represent the broadcast, allowing a third person to enjoy these rights or to oppose what she enjoys. The author meanwhile maintains his moral rights. In the countries of "Common Law", including the USA, a formal authorization or transfer of ownership in a written agreement is required.

In conclusion, it is usually best to clarify issues of copyright ownership in the original agreement and/or to make sure the copyright over the trademark is formally assigned to your company.

B. Mark created by an employee of the enterprise

A work created by an employee is a work created by an author under a contract of employment. The ownership of such works is treated differently depending on national legislation. In some countries such as England, Sweden, the USA and other countries of the "Common Law", these creations belong to the employer. In other countries however, such as France, Cameroon, Nigeria, they belong to the employee, unless otherwise stipulated in the contract.

It is important to clarify issues of copyright ownership before using the mark.

Annex I – Useful websites

For more information on:

Intellectual property issues from a business perspective: www.wipo.int/sme

Trademarks in general: www.wipo.int/about-ip www.inta.org (International Trademark Association)

The practical aspects relating to the registration of trademarks see Annex II or www.wipo.int/directory/en/urls.jsp

Madrid system for the International Registration of Marks www.wipo.int/madrid

International Classification of Goods and Services for the Purposes of the Registration of Marks under the Nice Agreement www.wipo.int/classifications (under Nice Agreement)

International Classification of the Figurative Elements of Marks under the Vienna Agreement www.wipo.int/classifications (under Vienna Agreement)

The conflict between trademarks and domain names and on alternative dispute resolution procedures for domain names www.arbiter.wipo.int/domains www.icann.org .

A list of the online trademark databases maintained by industrial property offices throughout the world is available at www.arbiter.wipo.int/trademark

Annexe II : Internet adresses of National and Regional Intellectual Property offices

For more information about the registration process .

African Intellectual Property Organization	www.oapi.wipo.net
Algeria	www.inapi.org
Albania	www.alpto.gov.al
Andorra	www.ompa.ad
Argentina	www.inpi.gov.ar
Armenia	www.armpatent.org
Australia	www.ipaustralia.gov.au
Austria	www.patent.bmvit.gv.at
Bahrain	www.gulf-patent-office.org.sa/bahrainframe.htm
Barbados	www.caipo.org
Belarus	www.belgospatent.or

g/english/about/history.html	
Belgium	www.mineco.fgov.be
Belize	www.belipo.bz
Benelux	www.boip.int
Benin	www.oapi.wipo.net
Bolivia	www.senapi.gov.bo
Botswana	www.aripo.org
Brazil	www.inpi.gov.br
Bulgaria	www.bpo.bg
Burkina Faso	www.oapi.wipo.net
Burundi	www.oapi.wipo.net
Cambodia	www.moc.gov.kh
Cameroon	www.oapi.wipo.net
Canada	www.opic.gc.ca
Central African Republic	www.oapi.wipo.net
Chad	www.oapi.wipo.net
Chile	www.dpi.cl
China	www.sipo.gov.cn
China (Hong Kong - SAR)	www.ipd.gov.hk
China (Macao)	www.economia.gov.mo

China (Marks)	www.saic.gov.cn
Colombia	www.sic.gov.co
Congo	www.oapi.wipo.net
Costa Rica	www.registronacional.go.cr
Côte d'Ivoire	www.oapi.wipo.net
Croatia	www.dziv.hr
Cuba	www.ocpi.cu
Cyprus	www.mcit.gov.cy/mcit/drcor/drcor.nsf
Czech Republic	www.upv.cz
Democratic Republic of the Congo	www.oapi.wipo.net
Denmark	www.dkpto.dk
Dominican Republic	www.seic.gov.do/onapi
Egypt	www.egypo.gov.eg
El Salvador	www.cnr.gobs.sv
Estonia	www.epa.ee
Eurasian Patent Office	www.eapo.org
European Union (Office for	Harmonizationin the

Internal Market – OHIM)	www.oami.eu.int
Finland	www.prh.fi
France	www.inpi.fr
Gabon	www.oapi.wipo.net
Gambia	www.aripo.org
Georgia	www.sakpatenti.org.ge
Germany	www.dpma.de
Ghana	www.aripo.org
Greece	www.obi.gr
Honduras	www.sic.gob.hn/pintelec/indice.htm
Hungary	www.mszh.hu/english/index.html
Iceland	www.patent.is/focal/webguard.nsf/key2/indexeng.html
India	www.ipindia.nic.in
Indonesia	www.dgip.go.id
Ireland	www.patentsoffice.ie
Israel	www.justice.gov.il
Italy	www.uibm.gov.it

Jamaica	www.jipo.gov.jm
Japan	www.jpo.go.jp
Jordan	www.mit.gov.jo
Kazakhstan	www.kazpatent.org/english
Kenya	www.aripo.org
Kuwait	www.gulf-patent-office.org.sa
Lao People's Democratic Republic	www.stea.la.wipo.net
Latvia	www.lrpv.lv
Lebanon	www.economy.gov.lb
Lesotho	www.aripo.org
Liechtenstein	www.european-patent-office.org
Lithuania	www.vpb.lt
Luxembourg	www.etat.lu/ec
Malawi	www.aripo.org
Malaysia	www.mipc.gov.my
Mali	www.oapi.wipo.net
Mexico	www.impi.gob.mx
Monaco	www.european-patent-

office.org/patlib/count	ry/monaco
Montenegro	www.yupat.sv.gov.yu
Morocco	www.ompic.org.ma
Mozambique	www.aripo.org
Namibia	www.aripo.org
Nepal	www.ip.np.wipo.net
Netherlands	www.octrooicentrum.nl
New Zealand	www.iponz.govt.nz
Niger	www.oapi.wipo.net
Norway	www.patentstyret.no
Oman	www.gulf-patent-office.org.sa
Panama	www.digerpi.gob.pa
Peru	www.indecopi.gob.pe
Philippines	www.ipophil.gov.ph
	Poland
	www.business.gov.pl/Intellectual,property,protection,90.html
Portugal	www.inpi.pt
Qatar	www.gulf-patent-office.org.sa

Republic of Korea	www.kipo.go.kr
Republic of Moldova	www.agepi.md
Romania	www.osim.ro
Russian Federation	www.rupto.ru
Saint Vincent and the Grenadines	196.1.161.62/govt/cipo/index.asp
Saudi Arabia	www.gulf-patent-office.org.sa
Senegal	www.oapi.wipo.net
Serbia	www.yupat.sv.gov.yu
Sierra Leone	www.aripo.org
Singapore	www.ipos.gov.sg
Slovak Republic	www.indprop.gov.sk
Slovenia	www.uil-sipo.si/Default.htm
Somalia	www.aripo.org
South Africa	www.cipro.gov.za
Spain	www.oepm.es
Sudan	www.aripo.org
Swaziland	www.aripo.org
Sweden	www.prv.se
Switzerland	www.ige.ch
Syrian Arab Republic	www.himaya.net

Tajikistan	www.tipat.org
Thailand	www.ipthailand.org
The Former Yugoslav Republic of Macedonia	www.ippo.gov.mk
Togo	www.oapi.wipo.net
Trinidad and Tobago	www.ipo.gov.tt/home.asp
Tunisia	www.inorpi.ind.tn
Turkey	www.turkpatent.gov.tr
Turkmenistan	www.eapo.org
Uganda	www.aripo.org
Ukraine	www.sdip.gov.ua
United Arab Emirates	www.gulf-patent-office.org.sa
United Kingdom	www.patent.gov.uk
United Republic of Tanzania	www.aripo.org
United States	www.uspto.gov
Uruguay	www.dnpi.gub.uy
Uzbekistan	www.patent.uz

Venezuela www.sapi.gov.ve
Yemen www.most.org.ye
Zambia www.aripo.org
Zimbabwe www.aripo.org

For up-to-date information visit website at the following urls: www.wipo.int/members/en/ and www.wipo.int/directory/en/urls.jsp 27

Annex III – Nice Classification: International Classification of Goods and Services for the Purposes of the Registration of Marks under the Nice Agreement

Goods

1. Chemicals used in industry, science and photography, as well as in agriculture, horticulture and forestry; unprocessed artificial resins, unprocessed plastics; manures; fire extinguishing compositions; tempering and soldering preparations; chemical substances for preserving foodstuffs; tanning substances; adhesives used in industry.

2. Paints, varnishes, lacquers; preservatives against rust and against deterioration of wood; colorants; mordents; raw natural resins; metals in foil and powder form for painters, decorators, printers and artists.

3. Bleaching preparations and other substances for laundry use; cleaning, polishing, scouring and abrasive preparations; soaps; perfumery, essential oils, cosmetics, hair lotions; dentifrice.

4. Industrial oils and greases; lubricants; dust absorbing, wetting and binding compositions; fuels (including motor spirit) and illuminants; candles and wicks for lighting.

5. Pharmaceutical and veterinary preparations; sanitary preparations for medical purposes; dietetic substances adapted for medical use, food for babies; plasters, materials for dressings; material for stopping teeth, dental wax; disinfectants; preparations for destroying vermin; fungicides, herbicides.

6. Common metals and their alloys; metal building materials; transportable buildings of metal; materials of metal for railway tracks; non-electric cables and wires of common metal; ironmongery, small items of metal hardware; pipes and tubes of metal; safes; goods of common metal not included in other classes; ores.

7. Machines and machine tools; motors and engines (except for land vehicles); machine coupling and transmission components (except for land vehicles); agricultural implements other than hand- operated; incubators for eggs.

8. Hand tools and implements (hand-operated); cutlery; side arms; razors.

9. Scientific, nautical, surveying, photographic, cinematographic, optical, weighing, measuring, signaling, checking (supervision), life-saving and teaching apparatus and instruments; apparatus and instruments for conducting, switching, transforming, accumulating, regulating or controlling electricity; apparatus for recording, transmission or reproduction of sound or images; magnetic data carriers, recording discs; automatic vending machines and mechanisms for coin-operated apparatus; cash registers, calculating machines, data processing equipment and computers; fire- extinguishing apparatus.

10. Surgical, medical, dental and veterinary apparatus and instruments, artificial limbs,

eyes and teeth; orthopedic articles; suture materials.

11. Apparatus for lighting, heating, steam generating, cooking, refrigerating, drying, ventilating, water supply and sanitary purposes.

12. Vehicles; apparatus for locomotion by land, air or water.

13. Firearms; ammunition and projectiles; explosives; fireworks.

14. Precious metals and their alloys and goods in precious metals or coated therewith, not included in other classes; jewelry, precious stones; horological and chronometric instruments.

15. Musical instruments.

16. Paper, cardboard and goods made from these materials, not included in other classes; printed matter; bookbinding material; photographs; stationery; adhesives for stationery or household purposes; artists' materials; paint brushes; typewriters and office requisites (except furniture); instructional and teaching material (except apparatus); plastic materials for packaging

(not included in other classes); printers' type; printing blocks.

17. Rubber, gutta-percha, gum, asbestos, mica and goods made from these materials and not included in other classes; plastics in extruded form for use in manufacture; packing, stopping and insulating materials; flexible pipes, not of metal.

18. Leather and imitations of leather, and goods made of these materials and not included in other classes; animal skins, hides; trunks and travelling bags; umbrellas, parasols and walking sticks; whips, harness and saddlery.

19. Building materials (non-metallic); non-metallic rigid pipes for building; asphalt, pitch and bitumen; non-metallic transportable buildings; monuments, not of metal.

20. Furniture, mirrors, picture frames; goods (not included in other classes) of wood, cork, reed, cane, wicker, horn, bone, ivory, whalebone, shell, amber, mother-of-pearl, meerschaum and substitutes for all these materials, or of plastics.

21. Household or kitchen utensils and containers (not of precious metal or coated therewith); combs and sponges; brushes (except paint brushes); brush-making materials; articles for cleaning purposes; steelwool; unworked or semi-worked glass (except glass used in building); glassware, porcelain and earthenware not included in other classes.

22. Ropes, string, nets, tents, awnings, tarpaulins, sails, sacks and bags (not included in other classes); padding and stuffing materials (except of rubber or plastics); raw fibrous textile materials.

23. Yarns and threads, for textile use.

24. Textiles and textile goods, not included in other classes; bed and table covers.

25. Clothing, footwear, headgear.

26. Lace and embroidery, ribbons and braid; buttons, hooks and eyes, pins and needles; artificial flowers.

27. Carpets, rugs, mats and matting, linoleum and other materials for covering existing floors; wall hangings (non-textile).

28. Games and playthings; gymnastic and sporting articles not included in other classes; decorations for Christmas trees.

29. Meat, fish, poultry and game; meat extracts; preserved, dried and cooked fruits and vegetables; jellies, jams, compotes; eggs, milk and milk products; edible oils and fats.

30. Coffee, tea, cocoa, sugar, rice, tapioca, sago, artificial coffee; flour and preparations made from cereals, bread, pastry and confectionery, ices; honey, treacle; yeast, baking-powder; salt, mustard; vinegar, sauces (condiments); spices; ice.

31. Agricultural, horticultural and forestry products and grains not included in other classes; live animals; fresh fruits and vegetables; seeds, natural plants and flowers; foodstuffs for animals, malt.

32. Beers; mineral and aerated waters and other non-alcoholic drinks; fruit drinks and fruit juices; syrups and other preparations for making beverages.

33. Alcoholic beverages (except beers).

34. Tobacco; smokers' articles; matches.

Services

35. Advertising; business management; business administration; office functions.

36. Insurance; financial affairs; monetary affairs; real estate affairs.

37. Building construction; repair; installation services.

38. Telecommunications.

39. Transport; packaging and storage of goods; travel arrangement.

40. Treatment of materials.

41. Education; providing of training; entertainment; sporting and cultural activities.

42. Scientific and technological services and research and design relating thereto; industrial analysis and research services; design and development of computer hardware and software; legal services.

43. Services for providing food and drink; temporary accommodation.

44. Medical services; veterinary services; hygienic and beauty care for human beings

or animals; agriculture, horticulture and forestry services.

45. Personal and social services rendered by others to meet the needs of individuals; security services for the protection of property and individuals.

In January 2006, 73 states were party to the Nice Agreement. They have adopted and apply the Nice Classification for the purposes of the registration of marks.

For up-to-date information, visit website at the following urls: www.wipo.int/classifications/fulltext/nice8/enmain.htm

and www.wipo.int/madrid/en/contact.html

Bibliography

Bentley Lionel & Sherman Brad, 2009, *Intellectual Property Law*, Oxford University Press

Cornish, LLewelyn and Aplin, 2010, Intellectual Property: Patents, copyright, trademarks, and allied rights, Sweet & Maxwell P 655

Toso Francesca (2012), *Handmade in Thailand: building brands for local communities*, WIPO Magazine, No5, 8-12

World Intellectual Property Organisation (WIPO)**,** 2008, *WIPO Intellectual Property Handbook*, **WIPO Publication N°489** (E)

P.O Box 35512 Yaounde/Cameroon

www.facebook.com/ipsaorg

ipsaorganisation@gmail.com

Contact us for:

- ➢ Registration of your trademark or service mark in Africa
- ➢ Consulting and mentoring

www.ingramcontent.com/pod-product-compliance
Lightning Source LLC
Chambersburg PA
CBHW071802200526
45167CB00017B/1069